COLONIAL

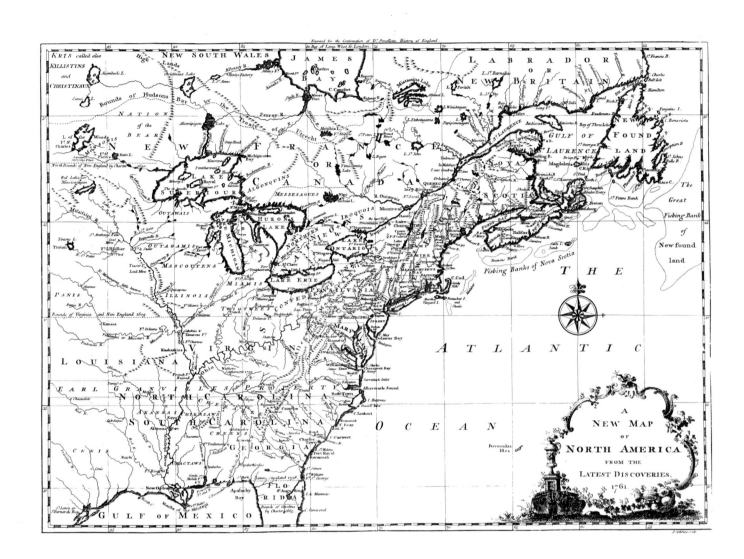

COLONIAL

DESIGN
IN THE NEW WORLD

DAVID LARKIN

JUNE SPRIGG & JAMES JOHNSON

PHOTOGRAPHS BY
MICHAEL FREEMAN & PAUL ROCHELEAU

STEWART
TABORI & CHANG
NEW YORK

A DAVID LARKIN BOOK

Text copyright © 1988 June Sprigg and James Johnson
Photographs copyright © 1988 Michael Freeman
Photographs copyright © 1988 Paul Rocheleau
Due to limitations of space, photo credits appear
on page 270 and constitute an extension of this page.

Published in 1988 by
Stewart, Tabori & Chang, Inc.
740 Broadway, New York, New York 10003

Library of Congress Cataloging-in-Publication Data

Larkin, David.
   Colonial : design in the new world / David Larkin, June Sprigg &
James Johnson ; photographs by Michael Freeman & Paul Rocheleau.—
1st ed.
      p.   cm.
   "A David Larkin book."
   Includes index.
   ISBN 1-55670-043-1
   1. Architecture, Domestic—United States.   2. Architecture,
Colonial—United States.   I. Sprigg, June.   II. Johnson, James,
1941–   .   III. Title.
NA707.L37   1988   88-15299
728′.0974—dc19   CIP

Distributed by Workman Publishing
708 Broadway, New York, New York 10003

Printed in Japan

10 9 8 7 6 5 4 3 2 1

CONTENTS

COLONIAL STYLE

preceding pages:

Colonial Americans settled on the edge of the New World. To the east lay more than three thousand miles of ocean, and the distant shores of their old home. To the west lay wilderness, and no one knew how far it went. Beyond the front door was an unknown land, "a plain wilderness as God first made it," in the words of Capt. John Smith. Yet this bleak landscape was also the source of sustenance—game, fish, crops, wood for fuel and building, fresh water—which gave the settlers what they needed to begin a life independent of the world they had left behind.

This central-chimney house was built in 1725 on Hog Island near Ipswich, Massachusetts, by Francis Choate. Choate's father, Thomas, had built his house nearby in 1690; a prosperous landowner who owned six farms, he was called "the Governor." In 1725, the elder Choate moved back to the mainland; his house was taken down sometime during the Revolution. Altogether, eighty children were born on Hog Island between 1690 and the very early nineteenth century. The exterior of this house remains almost exactly as it was built.

You are standing at the dock. Sea birds wheel overhead. Your journey began when the place you knew as home vanished from view. You are with some of those closest to you, but many more stayed behind. You will never see them again.

You are leaving because you believe that it will be better in the new world, that you will be able to have what you want most—religious freedom, adventure, a more prosperous life, or land. You live in an agricultural age. Land means wood and warmth, food and clothing for you and your family.

You are full of hope and fear. The ocean voyage will be long and dangerous. You have had to leave most of your material possessions behind. You have been able to bring with you only clothing and a small chest or barrel with the things you will need most.

But you bring with you something more. Imagine it as a blueprint of all the things you know—how to build, when to sow, how to assist at birth, how to worship, how to make a chair, how to govern. The experience and expectations of many generations go with you.

You miss your old home, no matter how much you want to leave it. You will see a red-breasted bird in the new world and give it the name of a bird you used to see back home. You will recognize the plants that ease pain or stop a cough, or you will find others that work as well. You will call your new home by an old name. You will take with you what you prize the most and leave the rest behind.

You are willing to risk all for a life in this new world. The crowd begins to move, and you walk aboard the ship.

AMERICA'S colonial history began in the early 1600s and ended with the Declaration of Independence. It lasted more than one hundred fifty years, enough time for six generations to be born. During that time the New World changed enormously. The colonists pressed the frontier inland, though not more than a couple of hundred miles by 1776. The colonies ran like a river north and south, the thinnest eastern rind of an unexplored continent. Rivers were highways; the rich land of the river valleys provided sustenance and prosperity.

The American colonists brought their familiar traditions from England and Europe, including how they lived, worked, and worshiped. They also re-created, as much as they could, the traditional ways of building houses, barns, and fences. Shelter was the immediate need. Doing what they had done back home was the quickest, most practical way to establish themselves and provide for their needs.

The look of familiar things also provided a link with the Old World, some 3,000 miles distant. The timber-framed houses built in Massachusetts in the first century of settlement were essentially English in both structure and appearance. A chest made of wood from a New World forest was designed in the style of the Old World. Joiners, turners, cabinetmakers, blacksmiths, and weavers had no need to create a new look for a new home. Seventeenth-century New England furniture looked English because the settlers here had come primarily from England. In New York, immigrants from Holland showed their background in houses and furniture that looked Dutch, such as the *kaas*, or large wardrobe. Germans in Pennsylvania brought traditions that included red clay roof tiles and plank-seat chairs.

With the passage of time and the establishment of prosperous households, settlers in American colonies quickly revealed their desire for style. Colonists knew what was stylish from their recollections of the Old World, as well as from fashionable furnishings imported by the well-to-do or from furniture made in America by cabinetmakers trained in Old World workshops. What was fashionable in Europe, however, generally did not make an appearance in the colonies until a decade or two later.

The earliest styles in colonial America are named for English monarchs. The basic style in the seventeenth century is sometimes called Jacobean, after James I, who reigned from 1603 to 1625. Because they came from a variety of sources, however, things made in this period may simply be called seventeenth-century. William and Mary were on the throne from 1689 to 1702 (William alone after Mary's death in 1694); the style now known as William and Mary was fashionable in America from about 1700 to 1725. The style known as Queen Anne (she reigned from 1702 to 1714) flourished here from about 1725 to 1755.

The next style in America is named for a fashionable English designer, Thomas Chippendale, who published his trend-setting furniture pattern book in 1754. The Chippendale style was popular here from about 1755 to 1780.

Seventeenth-century rooms had low ceilings and were dimly lit through small casement windows. The timber framing was exposed and usually whitewashed. Seventeenth-century furniture was heavy, blocklike, and rectilinear. What made it delightful to look at was the applied painted and carved decoration. Forms that were stylish included court cupboards, trestle tables, and turned great chairs with arms and high backs.

William and Mary furniture was characterized by strong curves and bold, detailed turnings. Marked color contrasts—red and black, yellow and green—were considered pleasing to the eye. Gate-leg tables, easy chairs, or wing chairs, and tall side chairs with caned backs and seats were popular.

Furniture in the Queen Anne style represented a dramatic change. Instead of massive forms and an emphasis on applied decoration, long, gracefully curved lines became the fundamental characteristic of style. Furniture was lighter and more delicate. The curved cabriole leg became very popular on chairs, beds, tea tables, and case pieces. The high chest, introduced in the William and Mary period, now came into wide use. Some of the influence of the Queen Anne style carried over into the Chippendale period. Furniture became more richly ornamental. Nothing looked more fashionable to the sophisticated eye than the claw-and-ball foot.

Building styles also linked the Old World to the New. Most of the houses built in the colonies in the first century of settlement closely resembled houses in England. The settlers raised structures with massive timber frames, then filled in the walls with wattle and daub, a combination of clay and interwoven saplings. These houses were added to throughout the century. Many of them have a strong medieval appearance, with steep gables, overhangs, and ornamental drops. At the same time, a uniquely American form of house was developing: the so-called salt-box house, which is characterized by the integration of a lean-to, or shed addition, into the original structure.

Early in the 1700s, new architectural influences were introduced. Façades became more important; the exterior became an integrated and logical design, balanced and symmetrical. This new style, which had roots in the Classical architecture of the Greeks and Romans, also featured ornament inside and out, on doors, windows, staircases, mantelpieces, and cornices. By the middle of the eighteenth century, fashionable houses were being built in the Georgian style (named for the English monarchs who reigned at the time). Interiors were characterized by bigger rooms and larger windows.

The story of the colonial period is the story of a journey from a crowded dock to a new nation ready to declare its independence. The houses and furnishings that have survived are documents we can read. They tell us not only about style, but also about the people who made or used them. Embellishment beyond utility—an expenditure of time made visible in carving or painted decoration—signifies something special, something the original owners felt proud to possess. We can see that a chest was made for a wedding gift because it has the initials of the newly married couple. A wrought-iron flesh fork for the kitchen that terminates in the shape of a heart *looks* as if it was a special present. The chair made for Governor Brewster *looked* like a seat worthy of his elevated place in society. A woman who spent most of her sewing time darning or mending would understandably lavish care on the embroidered bed hangings that she would make once in a lifetime.

The development of a distinctively American style of building and furniture-making took place as the colonies matured. In the seventeenth century, the main difference between English and American styles was simplification, in part because of the very small number of highly skilled craftsmen among the earliest settlers. In the eighteenth century, American styles were further removed from the original English sources. And with each new generation of American-born colonists, the ties grew weaker.

American furniture-makers rethought traditional Old World forms to accommodate the tastes and needs of their customers. Strong regional styles developed in America. It is often possible to identify the place of origin of a piece based on stylistic characteristics.

This book traces the development of American styles from the early seventeenth century through the years just before the Revolution. These houses, barns, chairs, and other creations are our visible reminders of the richness and diversity of the people who settled the colonies of the New World.

NEW ENGLAND

THE story of the first enduring settlement in New England is as familiar as pumpkin pie. In the fall of 1620, a hundred and one people spent ten weeks crossing the Atlantic in a crowded ship, arriving near what is now Provincetown, Massachusetts, in December. Five weeks later, they stepped ashore at a place they called Plimoth.

They came here for many reasons. Most of them came to practice their Separatist faith, prohibited by the church in England. Others were farmers, tradesmen, and other men and women without the Separatist convictions of the Pilgrims. Nearly half of them died the first winter, but the next year a new ship arrived, and settlers kept coming. By 1627, the community was largely self-supporting.

By that time, other newcomers had established a dozen other settlements along the Massachusetts coastline. Many of these settlers were Puritans, who were also at odds with the Church of England but who advocated reform from within. In 1629, they obtained a royal charter to form the Massachusetts Bay Colony.

Within twenty years after the landing of the *Mayflower*, there were about 20,000 settlers in New England, most of them in the Massachusetts Bay Colony. They included university graduates, clergy, rural laborers, tradesmen, farmers, fishermen, and woodsmen. Most arrived in groups led by their ministers, but not all came for high-minded reasons. When asked by his exasperated minister why he had come, one colonist in Portsmouth, New Hampshire, is said to have replied, "Us'n came to fish 'n' trade."

In 1630, Boston was established and named for a Lincolnshire town. It soon became the center of New England. Within a few years it was an important trading center, and by 1636 it could boast of Harvard College (although it was dismissed by an English commissioner as a mere "wooden colledge," and sniffed at by Dutch visitors from New Amsterdam, who said it smelled like a tavern).

Boston soon became the jumping-off place for settlers who wanted to move on. In 1636 Thomas Hooker left with a hundred followers and 160 cattle, as well as pigs and goats, and traveled over Indian trails to what became known as Connecticut. The same year, Roger Williams went to Rhode Island, where he founded a community called Providence as a haven for people who believed in the separation of church and state and who wished to live according to their own beliefs. Settlers moved quickly up the Connecticut River and along the Atlantic coastline. By 1640 there were 8,000 settlers in Connecticut alone. Within ten years there were dozens of towns both north and south of Boston.

Life in New England was highly ordered. Typically, towns were laid out around a common or green. Settlers cultivated their fields beyond the edges of town. Beyond the fields was pasture, and beyond that the woods. In part, New England colonists were reproducing the town plans familiar to them from English villages, but there was another, stronger reason to cluster in towns: the threat of Indian attack. Of ninety towns in New England, fifty-two had been attacked and twelve destroyed by the late seventeenth century. What happened to Deerfield, Massachusetts, terrified other settlers. There, residents were massacred not once but twice—once in 1675, during King Philip's War, and again in 1704, when some survivors were forced to march to Montreal in winter as hostages.

Town life centered around the meetinghouse and the school-house. Education was important for religious reasons; to be a church member, one had to be able to read the Bible. In 1647, the general court of the Massachusetts Bay Colony directed each town with more than fifty householders to appoint and pay a teacher. Later in the colonial period, most towns also had a tavern and a town hall.

Industry developed along with the towns. As early as 1623, Dover, New Hampshire, had a sawmill. Shortly after the mid-seventeenth century, there were twenty sawmills and a dozen shipyards along the Piscataqua River in New Hampshire. Along the coast, shipping and commerce flourished. By 1671, colonial seaports were exporting shiploads of boards, staves, masts, cod, and beaver pelts. With the success of every new enterprise, the New England colonies were a step closer to economic self-sufficiency.

All activities in New England—farming, fishing, manufacturing, traveling—were regulated by the climate. In spite of the claims of one early booster, whose 1630 pamphlet touted the "Temper of the Aire of New-England" and claimed that "a sup of New-England Aire is better than a whole draught of old Englands Ale," winters were hard and long. Rivers and harbors froze; mills closed. Families who made their living by farming turned their hands to other work.

As the number of settlers grew, the look of New England changed. Cultivated land replaced virgin forest. Bustling ports appeared on formerly quiet shores. To Old World eyes, New England's forests seemed a boundless resource. The abundance of this wood shaped New England. Its most important immediate use was for shelter. Most seventeenth-century colonists built small houses, with a hall, or common living area, beneath a chamber, or sleeping space, with a hearth and chimney at one side. As time passed and households grew, many New Englanders added two more rooms, a parlor below and a second chamber above, on the other side of the chimney. Many houses that eventually became much larger started as four rooms around a central chimney. These houses were built on post-and-beam frames, raised into place and then covered with clapboards or sheathing. The very first roofs at Plimoth were thatched, but within a few years wooden shingles came into use.

Seventeenth-century New England houses looked medieval, with their steeply pitched roofs, small windows, and second-story overhangs with ornamental drops. The rooms were simple and dimly lit. Inside, the timber-framed walls were infilled with wattle and daub or lath and plaster, leaving the beams exposed. Large hearths had rudimentary mantels at best. There was no built-in storage space, so the family's belongings were within sight and reach.

In the early eighteenth century, another floor plan evolved: a hallway in the center flanked by two smaller chimneys. Façades were symmetrical, with large windows framing a central entrance. Interior woodwork became a stylistic element. Ornamental paneling and classical details dressed up walls, ceilings, fireplaces, doors, windows, and cornices. By the end of the colonial period, some houses boasted decorated wallpaper, imported from England, China, or France.

The colonists who came to New England brought English and European furniture traditions with them. Throughout the colonial period, styles continued to evolve from Old World sources. In 1660, Boston had joiners, turners, and upholsterers.

Many chair makers and cabinetmakers were also at work. Later in the century, they were joined by other specialists: carvers, japanners, chair caners, picture frame carvers, and looking-glass makers. In 1751, a visitor from the West Indies declared that "the Artificers in the Place Exceed Any upon ye Continent." Massachusetts furniture styles were slow to change and relatively restrained, to suit a conservative clientele.

Other areas developed their own distinctive furniture styles. Newport, Rhode Island, was an important style center. There, three generations of the Goddard and Townsend families made furniture in the Queen Anne and Chippendale styles. They and other makers were well known for their case furniture, made of imported mahogany, often with elegant block-front design.

Connecticut furniture makers, removed from Boston and Newport, developed styles of their own. Distinctive traditions of this area include the heart-and-crown motif on chairs from 1720 until well after the Revolution and the so-called Hadley chests with flowers carved in flat relief.

In rural areas and towns throughout New England, utility was the primary concern. Country furniture makers characteristically looked to the cities to see what was stylish, then simplified the forms. Country furniture was not without style, however. In fact, much of it is very pleasing to the modern eye because of its simplicity and originality.

The spirit of New England is visible today in colonial towns, houses, and furniture—a combination of independent thinking and restraint. Like the things they made, New Englanders had their roots in England but stripped away what did not suit them. Combining what they thought best of the old and the new, New Englanders created a distinctive world of their own.

In 1609, a group of Separatists, or dissidents from the Anglican church, left their home in Scrooby, England, for Holland and a climate of greater religious tolerance. For the Separatists, religion was a direct relationship between an individual and God. They believed that each man and woman should read and interpret the Bible, and they objected to the way the Anglican bishops interfered in this direct relationship. In 1620, the Separatists returned to England and embarked for the New World in a ship called the *Mayflower*.

Of the 101 passengers, more than half died in the first winter in New England. Life was harsh, and the need for food and shelter was predominant. By 1627, the Plimoth settlers had built a substantial village with dwellings, several common storehouses, shelters for livestock, and a fort—meetinghouse that dominated the settlement's single street.

Today, Plimoth Plantation is a reconstructed village three miles from the original site that portrays the life of the Plimoth settlers in 1627. The buildings are based on evidence from written accounts, archaeological finds, and similar surviving buildings in England and the Low Countries dating from the same time. The village's furnishings are accurate reproductions of the kinds of things the settlers brought from England or made here. The people who work here adopt the personalities, dress, and speech of actual historical figures who lived at Plimoth, including Miles Standish and Priscilla Alden.

22

This view shows one of Plimoth Plantation's two long houses, comprising two rooms and lofts joined by a through passage. These houses were the largest in the settlement. Built onto the back of this one is a hen cote, or coop.

Also visible are two kinds of chimneys. The long house in the foreground has the simplest kind of chimney, a smoke hole in the roof that can be covered with a shutter hinged at the bottom. In the house behind is a more developed chimney, built of wattle and daub on an oak frame, sheathed over with clapboards.

The houses were suited to the New England climate. The steep pitch of the roofs, a building tradition brought from the Old World, was well adapted to shed snow. Windows were small and few, to conserve heat. Open to the outside in warm weather, they were covered with oiled linen or paper in cold weather to keep out drafts but still bring in some light. At night and in the worst weather, interior shutters brought maximum warmth.

Life in Plimoth centered on the street that divided the two rows of houses. In warm weather, it was a place to work and to meet. The small stockadelike redoubt near the center of this view was a constant reminder of the possible dangers of attack in the New World. The redoubt enclosed several small cannon whose range just reached the entrance gates, a last line of defense should an attack occur.

Besides its human passengers, the *Mayflower* had also brought animals to the New World, including pigs, cattle, sheep, chickens, and geese, as well as dogs and cats. Here in the foreground are goats of what is now known as the San Clemente breed, purebred descendants of goats left on a California island in the seventeenth century. These small goats are very similar to those that came to Plimoth.

Many fences were necessary to prevent livestock from wandering into kitchen gardens or houses. The fences woven of sassafras saplings are very much like the wattle in the walls of buildings to which the claylike daub was applied.

Also visible here at the left are haystacklike piles of dried bundles of thatch, used for roofing. Other bundles of thatch just behind are drying against the wall.

Plimoth's thatcher had a most important job providing snug, waterproof roofs. Thatching is a skilled job with many steps. Bundles of thatch are held to the roof frame with horizontal wooden strips called liggers, "stapled" to the underlying layers with pointed, bent wooden spars. The three bundles of thatch at the roofline are called dolls and help to form the cap. In 1628, a fire scare prompted the Plimoth settlers to replace thatched roofs with more fire-resistant wooden shingles.

The thatcher's clothing is typical for a colonial man at work. He wears a hat, a shirt and doublet, knee breeches, stockings, and leather shoes. His breeches, red faded to pink, may seem surprisingly colorful, but the Plimoth settlers liked bright colors and wore them.

The thatcher prepares a ligger with his knife. Everything in Plimoth had to be prepared by hand; there were no mills or mechanization here as there were in the Old World.

30

Most of the produce that the Plimoth settlers raised was grown from seeds brought from the Old World. In addition, the settlers learned to use native Jerusalem artichokes, some kinds of pumpkins, and Indian corn—the familiar kerneled cobs, in contrast to what the English knew and still know as corn, the grains that we call wheat.

Bread was an important part of the Plimoth settlers'
meals. The settlement did not have a gristmill, so the
grain was milled into flour by hand, using a mortar and
pestle. Rye, Indian corn, and wheat were all used to
make bread. Yeast was available from brewing. Plimoth
women baked their loaves in communal outdoor clay
ovens; an oven in each house would have been too
much work to build, and too wasteful of firewood.

Fish from the ocean were part of the diet at Plimoth.
Here, a woman scales a fish. Other seafood eaten
in times of privation included lobsters, clams, and
mussels.

She is wearing a tasseled pocket for her personal
belongings, perhaps a handkerchief and paper of pins,
and a leather knife sheath. Knives, which had to be
imported from England, were valued because they were
needed for so many tasks.

Plimoth's thatched roofs were made of cattail rushes that grew along rivers and in marshes.

In actual practice, spreading thatch to dry was a muddy job that took place on the river banks. The work was traditionally done by men, who worked unclothed to spare their breeches; not many had extra clothing. Naturally, women stayed away for the sake of modesty.

The woman wears typical clothing of the period: a cap, a doublet (or jacket) over a shift, a full-length sleeved garment like a nightgown, a petticoat or skirt, an apron, stockings, and leather shoes. Clothes were made of linen and wool; cotton and silk, at this time, were luxurious fabrics for the prosperous.

A Plimoth settler prepares to thatch a small house called a hovel, dug about three feet into the ground. Such small, extremely simple dwellings were the first shelters built at Plimoth, and were based on similar dwellings in England and the Low Countries.

The hovel consists of three A-frames called crucks. The traditional curve, which allowed slightly more interior headroom, required men to venture into the forest to search for oaks with the proper natural curve. The pieces of the frame fit together like a giant puzzle, with joints formed of mortises (holes) and tenons (which fit into the holes), secured by wooden dowels or pegs.

The hovels may have been small, crowded, and exceedingly primitive, but no doubt they were dearly valued as the settlers' first homes on New World soil.

A hearth corner at Plimoth shows an attempt to bring convenience and some comfort to a work space. The built-in settle, or bench, provides a place to sit; the window is placed where it can bring light into the work area. The whitewashed daub wall helps reflect what natural daylight enters through the door and small window.

The area is typically furnished for the period. On the shelf are a wooden platter, a whisk broom, and a ceramic butter pot. Hanging from a hook on the wall is an iron-and-brass skimmer. On the floor are a brass kettle, andirons, a simple stool, a lidded iron pot, and a wooden boxlike foot warmer, in which a ceramic dish could hold coals to bring warmth to the feet.

Meals in most Plimoth houses were prepared on the hearth in a smoke bay. In this simplest kind of arrangement, there was no chimney, simply a hole in the roof through which the smoke ascended (see pages 26–27). Inside, the hearth is separated from the rest of the house by a wattle-and-daub partition. A piece of woolen blanket hangs in front of the hearth at the top to keep smoke from coming into the room. The light coming through the boards at the back of the smoke bay comes from the through passage of this long house.

This hearth is typically furnished with such equipment as a twig broom, wooden water pail, iron pot with short legs to stand it in the embers, trammel to suspend the pot above the fire, chopping block for splitting kindling, iron poker, small green blown-glass bottle, wooden bowl, earthenware bowl, and stoneware drinking pot.

The hearth was the center of life in winter, when the family gathered around the fire to keep warm. In warm weather, sunlight from the open door helped bring light into this dark interior.

44

It was with such equipment that William Bradford wrote *Of Plimoth Plantation* in 1627, still the best description of the settlement. Paper, which was highly valued, had to be imported from England. The settlers also bought ink, although they could make their own from walnut shells if necessary. Quills were made at home from the wing feathers of a goose, trimmed to a point with a knife. The ink pot was earthenware, imported from England. The writer forms his lines compactly, to economize on paper.

The Plimoth settlers prized literacy because they believed that people should read and interpret the Bible for themselves, not rely on the power of the church to give it to them. Writing formalized the agreements that enabled the settlers to live together harmoniously.

This English timber-framed house, which dates mainly
from the early fifteenth century, shows one of the
building traditions that English settlers brought to the
American colonies. It was built by a yeoman farmer in
the Weald region of East Sussex and Kent in southern
England. It has been restored and moved to the Weald
and Downland Open Air Museum in West Sussex,
England.

The steeply pitched roof and gables of the Iron Works House in Saugus, Massachusetts, recall English and European medieval building traditions. This large and impressive house was probably built in 1681 by Samuel Appleton, Jr., for his bride. Appleton was a gentleman farmer from a large landowning family in Ipswich. Although the house is named for the Iron Works, there is no direct connection; for all practical purposes the Iron Works ceased operations by 1670.

The gables, a typical feature of larger American houses at this time, added space and light to otherwise dark, cramped upper stories. The ornamental wooden pyramids or obelisks atop the gables were added when Wallace Nutting restored the house in 1915.

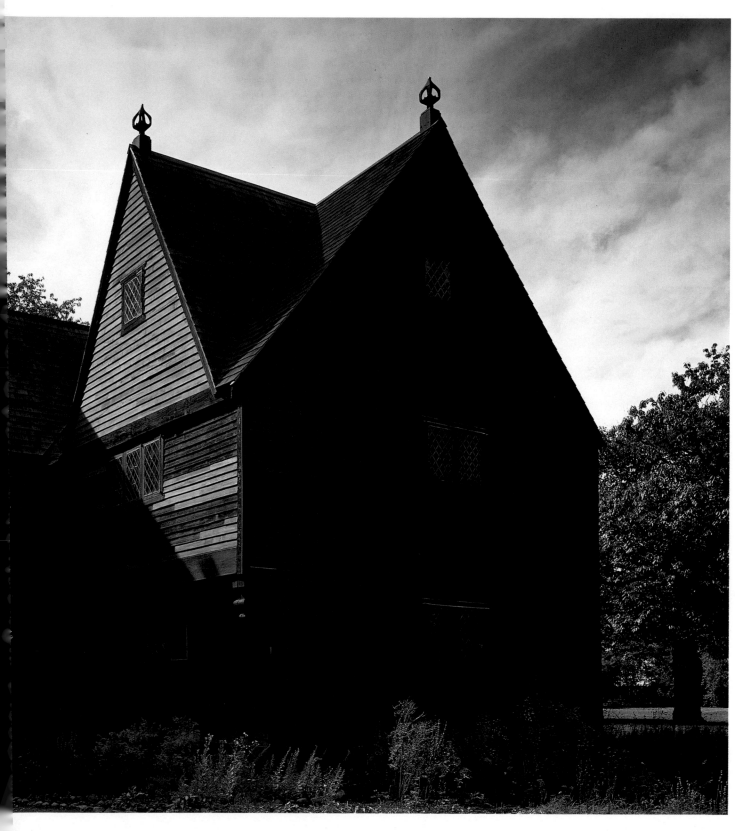

This central-chimney house, considered fine and substantial when it was built in 1683 for Parson Joseph Capen and his new wife, Priscilla, in Topsfield, Massachusetts, was the residence of the parson and his family for forty-two years. Typically, the downstairs included a hall, or kitchen, and a parlor flanking the chimney and stairs in the center of the house. In 1915, the local historical society restored the house in one of the early efforts in New England to preserve its architectural legacy.

preceding pages:

The home of Frances and Rebecca Nurse in Danvers, Massachusetts, is a classic salt-box shape: the roof extends low over a lean-to added to the back of the original house. The unfortunate Rebecca was hanged as a witch in 1692, one of the victims of the hysteria at that time in Salem and the surrounding area.

The term salt-box is used because the shape was reminiscent of the slanted lids of wooden boxes used earlier to store salt, a relatively precious commodity in the seventeenth century.

Also visible to the right of the house is a well sweep, a long pole used as a lever to lower and raise the pail in the well.

The house the Coffin family of Newbury, Massachusetts, built sometime around 1654 is a fine example of the way New Englanders expanded and updated their ancestral homes with the passage of generations, retaining the original house rather than tearing it down and building anew. Members of the original Coffin family lived in this house for more than two centuries before the Society for the Preservation of New England Antiquities acquired the property in 1929. The shape of the house is a visual record of the growth of a family.

Boldly carved wooden drops or pendants were a
decorative element on some seventeenth-century
houses. This example, on the Parson Capen House, is
unusual because it is squared, not bulbous. The house
is also distinguished by its having four drops, one at
each corner of the roof, not simply two in front as was
the common practice. These pendants have been
reproduced from other houses built during the same
period.

The door on the Parson Capen House in Topsfield,
Massachusetts, is a characteristic form of English door
used on both houses and churches as far back as the
medieval period. It is copied from a door of similar age
at Deerfield, Massachusetts. More than 150 massive
iron nails fasten three sturdy boards to another layer of
boards behind, laid in a different direction (either
diagonally or horizontally) for extra strength—the
same principle used to give strength to modern
plywood.

63

In order to create a more stylish façade, some builders in the eighteenth century carved wood to look like stone, dressing up the house by giving it the appearance of a more expensive building material. The technique was called rustication. The boards on the Porter-Phelps-Huntington House in Hadley, Massachusetts, were painted red-brown, possibly in imitation of Connecticut sandstone. The grooves between were painted white to imitate mortar.

The house is remarkable because it is the only known garrison-type dwelling (that is, one whose second story overhung the first) to have originally been rusticated. In a later remodeling, the rusticated boards and the overhang were concealed under clapboards.

Sometime around 1687, William Boardman of Saugus, Massachusetts, built a handsome central-chimney house with hall (or kitchen) and parlor on the ground floor and chambers above. By 1696, however, his family had the means and the need to add along the back a lean-to, divided into a bedroom, additional kitchen, and milk house, or dairy room.

This view of the wood-shingled roof shows the angle created at the juncture of the main roof and the less steeply pitched lean-to roof. It also shows how the lean-to kitchen's chimney flue adjoined the main chimney in a manner reminiscent of clustered brick chimneys in Tudor England. One or two original shingles remain on the roof underneath the shingles that are on the roof now. Although the original ones were hand-split, not machine-made, they are nearly as regular and even as the later shingles.

The hipped roof of the house on the Casey Farm in Saunderstown, Rhode Island, is most unusual. This remarkable house, built sometime around 1750, was home to generations of the Casey family for two centuries before it was bequeathed to the Society for the Preservation of New England Antiquities. The property remains a working farm.

This is grander than an ordinary farmhouse; for the Caseys, New England was a world of plenty. The landscape (although not the house itself) resembles a very substantial English yeoman's farm with its close-cropped open green land defined by stone walls.

The house is conceived as a whole, encased with façades on all sides that present a logical, orderly plan of windows, doors, and proportions in general, in marked contrast to the earlier building tradition, which simply added rooms as the need for them arose over time. Compare the tidiness of this house's overall appearance with the random growth of the Coffin House (see page 61).

This iron back, or cast back—now usually known as a fireback—is among the earliest examples of iron casting in the American colonies. Dated 1655 and bearing the initials of Edward Hutchinson, the probable owner, it was a product of the Iron Works in Saugus, Massachusetts. This fireback, which was installed at the back of a fireplace to protect the bricks from heat damage and reflect some heat into the room, is one of five in existence from the Iron Works.

Of stylistic interest is the pattern of decorative drops, or spindles, which closely resemble the turned wooden ornament on fine furniture from the same period. The resemblance is not coincidental, since the fireback (like cast-iron products in general) was made from a mold prepared by impressing carved wooden patterns into fine, damp casting sand.

The smoke oven in the Porter-Phelps-Huntington
House in Hadley, Massachusetts, is "up attic," in the
loft above the dining room. Sausages, bacon, hams, and
other cuts of meat were hung here to acquire the tang of
wood smoke, which also helped to dry and preserve them.

Early immigrants to the colonies usually brought only boxes or trunks that held their personal possessions. Carpenters and joiners were employed in large numbers in the mid-seventeenth century to build houses and furnish them. There are three chests around the walls of the parlor in the Iron Works House. All were made in America; two date from the seventeenth century, and one from the early eighteenth. The one-handed hanging clock on the wall was made in England in the late seventeenth century. The great chair is painted dark green with verdigris, and the forms, or benches, were used for seating at the long table.

This storage chest made circa 1700 is in the Thomas Lee House in Niantic, Connecticut. Instead of six boards joined to form a large box, this chest was made of a frame and panels.

While this type of chest originated in England, this particular example was made in America. The frame and panels are held together with wooden pins.

The crest of a banister-back side chair at the Parson Capen House in Topsfield, Massachusetts, was carved to commemorate "P. Capen" and the date 1708. It is believed that the chair was inscribed for Priscilla Capen, the parson's wife. It is not known why the date 1708 was commemorated, and it is thought that the inscription was added at a later date. The chair may have been assembled from parts of more than one chair at some time in the past.

The spindles show pleasing signs of age and wear in the places where they have been flattened, as a result of being placed against a wall throughout many years of use. The carved crest is chamfered, or trimmed at an angle, along the top edge to give it a thinner, lighter appearance from the front. The shape of the crest, as well as the name carved in it, is eerily reminiscent of gravestones of the same period.

The north chamber of the Sheldon-Hawks House in Deerfield, Massachusetts, includes some high-style furnishings. The bed is hung with a reproduction of the copperplate-printed fabric made in England in the eighteenth century. The pattern shows people playing blindman's buff. The curtains were hung by small brass rings from iron rods, for easy opening and closing. With the curtains drawn, the bed became a miniature room of its own, private and warm.

In front of the bed is a corner chair, the predecessor to the swivel chair. The chair did not swivel, but the sitter could.

Other furnishings include a leather-upholstered easy chair, or wing chair; a chest of drawers made in the Boston area; and a set of Jackfield ware, glossy black with gilt trim.

The convenient pantry shelves in the corner just off the kitchen (see pages 86–87) in the Wells-Thorn House in Deerfield, Massachusetts, exemplify the New England adage "A place for everything, and everything in its place." The pantry has been furnished with an accurate representation of the numbers and types of things stored in pantries in this area around 1725. This information was gleaned from probate inventories.

The contents include (from the top down) a pewter dish; dark-green blown-glass bottles, dated to this period; a pewter basin; treen, or turned wooden bowls and plates; a sieve; and a cast-iron kettle. The contents also point to the colonies' dependence on England and Europe for many goods. Here, only the treen and sieve could readily have been made locally.

The hall chamber of the Buttolph-Williams House in Wethersfield, Connecticut, traditionally thought to have been built sometime around 1692 by David Buttolph, has some of the finest original woodwork in the house. The bold, rounded bolection moldings around the fireplace are typical of the period. The fireplace's proportions—taller than wide—are typical of seventeenth-century houses. The raised hearth is typical of this region. The interior woodwork has been repainted to resemble a color of this period.

The fireplace is flanked by two similar but not identical heart-and-crown banister-back armchairs. This motif, at the top of the back on the crest, was typical of work from a small group of Connecticut furniture makers.

Parson Peter Smith built his house in South Windham, Maine, in 1764, when he married. Smith was a graduate of Harvard, and his father was a prominent minister in Portland for nearly seventy years. In spite of his distance from cities, he built an unexpectedly stylish home. The raised-panel fireplace wall with the convenient cupboards must have pleased his wife. Many colonial kitchens were painted yellow or ochre.

The flat, painted wooden figure by the hearth was known as a "silent companion." It was probably made in Boston, and is a fine example of this interesting and little-known home decoration. It was a gift from his mother-in-law, who also gave the couple a slave named Phyllis. The purpose of "silent companions" is not precisely clear, although some have whimsically suggested that they were for "company." The five-foot figure may have served as a fire screen, to protect a sitter from the direct heat of the fire, but is more than likely that she was mostly decorative. About a dozen such figures are known in America. They also include soldiers and animals in human dress.

Space-saving furnishings such as tilt-top tables, drop-leaf tables, and folding beds were considered useful. This "turn up," or press bedstead, now in the north kitchen of the Sheldon-Hawks House in Deerfield, Massachusetts, conveniently folds up against the wall when not in use, much as we use sofa beds today. (Colonial Americans referred to beds as bedsteads; the bed itself, to them, was the mattress.) The bedstead, made of maple and pine, was made in New England.

Like nearly all bedsteads of the colonial period, it is strung with rope that supported a mattress stuffed with straw, cornhusks, or feathers. When the ropes stretched periodically, causing the mattress to sag, a bed wrench was used to tighten them.

Inserting the wrench into the first long "stitch" of rope on the outside of the rails and twisting it made the rope tighten as the wrench took up the slack. By replacing the wrench with a wooden peg and moving to the next "stitch," the slack could continue to be taken up until each section was adjusted.

The south parlor of the Wells-Thorn House has been furnished with the things that were in parlors in this area around 1775, according to a study of household inventories. In the Connecticut River Valley, bedsteads were kept in parlors until the Revolution. Blue checked bed hangings were particularly popular in western Massachusetts. The bed is covered with a "rugg," or completely needleworked blanket, made by a young woman in Colchester, Connecticut, in the 1770s. Two chairs in the Queen Anne style are silhouetted against the windows. One is seated with splint, or split ash, and the other with "flagg," or rush.

The plain pine floor, without any finish at all, is also accurate to the period. Floors were scrubbed to keep them clean. Carpets were not regarded as necessities until the nineteenth century. One advantage of the unfinished pine boards was the way they reflected light. The decorative carved or turned legs of furniture in this period also showed to advantage against the light-colored floor.

The southwest chamber of the Sheldon-Hawks House is
small but comfortably furnished. The pieced calli-
manco, or glazed wool, coverlet on the bed adds color
and warmth. It was made in the late eighteenth
century. The vast majority of colonial women's needlework was what was known as plain sewing: mending,
patching, darning, hemming, and making garments
such as the white linen shift and shirt hanging on the
wall.

The banister-back side chair was a stylish form of seating in the late seventeenth and early to mid-eighteenth centuries. Such chairs were the work of artisans known as turners; the posts and back spindles were turned on a lathe. The bold ring and vase shapes in the posts are echoed in the spindles.

The flat side usually faces forward for more comfort. Although the seat is a replacement, the original also probably was made of twisted fibers of rush or cattail—an inexpensive, durable, and comfortable seat. This chair is at the Thomas Lee House in Niantic, Connecticut.

In 1771, Charles and Elizabeth Porter Phelps began to remodel the house that Elizabeth's father had built in 1752 in Hadley, Massachusetts. They hired Samuel Gaylord, Jr., to do the work. Almost all the rooms were originally paneled with vertical pine boards that were not painted. It is not yet clear whether this room originally had plastered walls, or whether this was part of the remodeling. The sliding shutter is original to the 1752 house.

In addition to redoing some woodwork, Gaylord also provided the Phelpses with some new furniture. The chair is one of a set of six banister chairs listed on a bill. (The term *banister* could also refer to what we call the back splat.)

The sword in the window recalls part of the family lore. When Moses Porter was killed during the French and Indian War in 1755, his Indian servant returned home and silently handed Porter's sword to his wife through the open window where she sat. The sword remains among the family belongings.

The handsomely paneled fireplace wall in the north parlor of the Sheldon-Hawks House in Deerfield, Massachusetts, dates from about 1743. It retains an early coat of paint. The Chippendale chair was made in Massachusetts around 1770. The looking-glass is probably American. Also of interest is the narrow mopboard, or baseboard, which was painted a mahogany color in contrast with the rest of the wall. The fireback in the fireplace bears an image of General James Wolfe, killed in 1759 in the French and Indian War—an English hero in the colonies.

The left door leads to the front entrance and main stair hall; the door on the far right goes into a passage behind the chimney. In between is a closet with shelves, or what we would probably call a built-in cupboard. Closets and similar built-in storage spaces were an uncommon convenience at the time this house was built.

Wallpaper was very rare in colonial America. It was all imported, whether printed or hand painted, French, English, or Chinese. The original red flocked wallpaper in the northeast bedchamber postdates the colonial period by a few years. It was applied in 1781, just before a visit by George Washington. The house was built thirty years earlier in Wethersfield, Connecticut, by Joseph Webb.

The lowboy, or dressing table, was probably made in the Boston area.

Like the glittering brass buttons on a stylish coat, shining brass drawer pulls decorated the front of high chests and chests-on-chests. They were imported from England and used on the most expensive furniture. This particular style, characterized by the bail handle and the intricately shaped plate, was popular throughout the 1700s. Dozens of variations of this basic shape were available. They were kept brightly polished to set them off against imported mahogany or native cherry or maple.

These brasses are on a high chest of drawers, made in the Hadley area circa 1770, in the Porter-Phelps-Huntington House in Hadley, Massachusetts.

preceding pages:

The parlor in the Silas Deane House, built in 1766 in Wethersfield, Connecticut, is elegant in its interior architecture and its furnishings. The handsome carved mantel is framed by the painted paneling that covers the fireplace wall. The mantel is probably made of Portland stone, from the quarry in Portland, Connecticut.

Furnishings include Chippendale chairs, made in Rhode Island, a tea table that belonged to the Deanes (on loan from the Connecticut Historical Society), a needleworked fire screen to protect a lady's fine white complexion from the intense heat of the fireplace, and a large Oriental carpet, the product of thousands of hours of handwork. Straight legs, which vary from plain to highly ornate, began to replace cabriole legs on Chippendale chairs in England about 1760. The portrait is of Silas Deane.

Some of the most charming furniture in the colonial period was made for children. The southwest chamber of the Sheldon-Hawks House in Deerfield, Massachusetts, includes a small slant-front writing desk with bun feet, and a child's banister-back chair.

The simple designs incised on a headstone for Thomas Avery in a Connecticut burying ground reveal the hand of a fairly unskilled worker. The floral scrolls in the columns on each side are particularly crude. The death's-head, however, has a certain stark power, reminding all observers of the inevitable outcome of being mortal. The stone mason, in addition to being relatively unskilled in terms of design and carving, also forgot to put the *h* in the word *who* and, having realized this, simply added it above.

The stone for young James Procter, only sixteen months old when he died, was carved by a skilled mason. The scrolls on each side are much more graceful than in the preceding example, and the angel's head is carved in high relief, not simply scratched into the stone's flat surface. The small stone on the right is probably the footstone to an adjacent grave.

Young James's stone reminds us how much higher was the incidence of childhood mortality in colonial America than it is here now. Rare indeed was the household unscarred by the loss of a child.

THE MIDDLE COLONIES

BETWEEN Virginia and New England lay the middle colonies: New York, New Jersey, Pennsylvania, Delaware, and Maryland. In contrast to early New England, this was a region of great cultural diversity. Settlers came from different parts of Europe, not just England, bringing with them many different cultural and religious traditions. In 1744, Dr. Alexander Hamilton, traveling through the colonies, stayed at a tavern in Philadelphia where he dined with twenty-five others in a "great hall well stoked with flys." His companions represented fifteen different backgrounds: "There were Scots, English, Dutch, Germans, and Irish; there were Roman Catholicks, Church men, Presbyterians, Quakers, Newlight men, Methodists, Seventh-day men, Moravians, Anabaptists, and one Jew." As early as 1629, a visitor reported hearing fourteen languages spoken in the streets of New Amsterdam (later New York). This diversity was not always seen as beneficial. According to one English observer, "Our chiefest unhappyness here is too great a mixture of nations, and the English the least part."

The history of the middle colonies begins in 1609, when the explorer Henry Hudson, sailing up the river he named for himself, claimed the Hudson and surrounding lands for the Netherlands. Within a few years, other explorers laid claim to the Connecticut and Delaware rivers and their environs for the Dutch. Only twelve years after Hudson's voyage, the colony of New Netherland was established. The first settlers arrived in 1623, when the Dutch West India Company sent thirty families led by Cornelius May to an island inhabited by the Manahatta tribe in the harbor of the Hudson River.

The harbor, the finest along the eastern coast, was a magnet for commerce-minded colonists. The Dutch West India Company had a single objective: to develop trade with the Indians, obtaining furs that it sold in Europe. An early shipment from New Amsterdam included 7,246 beaver skins, 853 otter pelts, and 151 skins of lynx, muskrat, and mink, as well as walnut and oak timber. Within a few years, New Amsterdam was the busiest port in the New World, with ships traveling from North America to the West Indies, Europe, and Africa.

In contrast to the New England colonies, which were settled originally by colonists seeking religious freedom, New York was primarily a commercial venture. While early New England settlers made the building of a meeting house the first priority, the first New Amsterdam settlers built a fort, a warehouse, a mill, and a meeting house—in that order. Soon there were more Dutch settlers in New York, New Jersey, and southern Connecticut.

There was no surge of colonists, however, because life in the Netherlands was good for most people, who enjoyed relative prosperity and a tolerant religious climate. To attract newcomers, the Dutch West India Company developed the idea of patroonships—vast tracts of land, up to 200,000 acres, tax-free for a decade—for anyone who could persuade fifty or more settlers to make the move. Patroonships were created along the rivers, either sixteen miles along one bank or eight miles along both banks, and as far back as the settlers wished to venture.

The concept sounded attractive. However, it soon became clear that the primary advantage belonged to the patroons, the men who obtained the patroonships. The desire for individual gain often outweighed concern for the settlers or for the Dutch West India Company. In violation of their agreement, some patroons established an illicit fur trade with New England, garnering the profits themselves instead of passing them on to the company. While the patroons grew rich, the settlers who farmed the patroons' land often did not fare so well. In addition, some patroons provoked trouble with the Indians by ignoring the company's policy of paying them for goods received, including land.

The Dutch were a major power in North America for only about fifty years. Beset by internal problems, the Dutch colony was not able to sustain its claim on the Connecticut River Valley and other important territory. Settlers from New England poured into the rich farmland of the Connecticut River Valley and onto Long Island. In 1664, New Amsterdam became New York following a peaceful takeover by the English. In 1673, the Dutch recaptured the city, but they lost it again to the English the following year. By the end of the colonial era in 1775, more than 25,000 people lived in New York City, a major center of commerce.

The Dutch also had troubles to the south. In 1638, a group of about fifty Swedish settlers established a community in what is now Delaware. Ironically, they were led by Peter Minuit, the first governor of New Amsterdam, who had fallen out of grace. After Minuit's death three years later, the Swedish monarch attempted to strengthen New Sweden—and improve society in Sweden— by sending to the community men who had evaded military duty or committed other crimes. They brought their families and were permitted to return home after one or two years if they wished. New Sweden never achieved major importance as a colony.

Pennsylvania was destined to become one of the most important colonies. It was the brainchild of William Penn, an Englishman, who received forty thousand square miles of land from King Charles as payment of a debt to Penn's father, the admiral of the English fleet. The colony's success was due in large part to Penn's commitment to peace with the natives, religious tolerance, and a fair chance for all. Pennsylvania was second only to Rhode Island in extending freedom of conscience to settlers. Promoted widely in Europe, the new colony attracted poor people from England, Scotland, Ireland, France, Germany, Holland, and Switzerland. It was a haven for Quakers, who were persecuted in the Old World and elsewhere in the New.

Settlement of Pennsylvania began in 1681 with three boatloads of Quakers. Within four years, more than 72,000 people had moved to Penn's colony. Most were German. In 1683, 43,000 acres were sold to a group of settlers who established Germantown.

The social, business, and style center of Pennsylvania was Philadelphia, which Penn called his "greene Countrie Towne." The new city was laid out in a grid pattern, influencing the design of later American cities. Citizens planted trees along the streets, which they named after the trees: Pine, Walnut, Chestnut, and others. Fine streets, pleasant homes, and busy piers and warehouses were all signs of a thriving ecomony and good government.

In the countryside beyond Philadelphia, rich farmland attracted more German settlers. Scotch-Irish pushed the frontier west. By the time of the Revolution, Pennsylvania was ready to take a leadership role in the formation of an independent nation.

Maryland was Pennsylvania's neighbor to the south. In 1632, King Charles II gave a large tract of land to George Calvert, whom the English king named Lord Baltimore. The colony consisted of present-day Maryland, Delaware, southern Pennsylvania, and much of West Virginia. The colony was intended primarily as a haven for English Catholics, who differed with the Anglican church on many issues. In 1634, about three hundred colonists landed on the shore of the Chesapeake Bay and established a settlement called St. Mary's. Charles II gave the colony an extraordinary amount of autonomy, including rights to create courts, appoint judges, set up trade, and coin currency.

The assembly's first action was to pass a law guaranteeing religious freedom to all settlers. In spite of Catholic dominance, other Christians were welcome. In 1649, Puritans in Virginia migrated to the new colony and settled on the site of what is now Annapolis.

The new inhabitants enjoyed the benefits of rich soil, abundance of fish and waterfowl, and a temperate climate. The first settlers engaged in farming small holdings, but soon turned to raising tobacco when they saw how successful Virginians were with that crop. The colony prospered under the beneficent rule of a succession of Lords Baltimore.

Later, however, Maryland's fortunes changed when Charles II attempted to outlaw manufacturing and split off all of what is now Delaware as a gift to his brother. By the Revolution, Maryland was significantly reduced in size, extending from the Potomac River to the Pennsylvania border.

Annapolis was the largest urban center in Maryland. It replaced St. Mary's as the capital in 1694. Today, the old part of the city retains the street plan drawn up by Royal Governor Francis

Nicholson. Streets radiate out from the State House, the oldest in the country in continuous use. Nicholson also designed the street plan for Williamsburg, Virginia, where, today, parallel streets—Francis and Nicholson—bear his name.

The diversity of cultures in the middle colonies was reflected in the houses and furnishings of the settlers. In the eighteenth century, Philadelphia became a major style center. By mid-century, when the Chippendale style was becoming fashionable, Philadelphia was producing large quantities of furniture in the new style. In 1755, Francis Trumble, a cabinetmaker, advertised twenty-three different types of furniture that he could make in a wide variety of woods, according to the customer's taste. The Library Company of Philadelphia, which was the public library, included among its holdings a copy of Thomas Chippendale's *Director*. Thomas Affleck, a well-known and highly skilled cabinetmaker, had a copy of his own. Like New York, Philadelphia was a stylish city that to many could have been a part of London.

The Germans in the New World carried on the traditions of northern Europe. They built homes, outbuildings, and furniture that had their origins in medieval antecedents. The first settlers built log cabins in the northern European style. These quickly gave way to substantial houses of fieldstone. Their barns were very large to house big dairy herds. Traditional German forms of furniture included the *schrank*, or large wardrobe, sometimes with drawers below, and the *ausschteier kischt*, or dower chest. A common form of seating was a simple chair with a plank seat, plank back with scalloped edges, and simple stick legs.

Some of the early furniture makers worked exclusively in Old World traditions, while others created furniture that was influenced by English and Continental styles—Queen Anne, Chippendale, and so on. But even among makers working in the fashionable styles, the earlier influences persisted, both in construction techniques and proportions.

Another characteristic of Swiss and German furniture was the use of decorative paint. Popular motifs included carnations, hearts, stars, birds, trees, flowers, tulips, unicorns, and human figures. Colonists of German origin were also fond of adding the names or initials of the owners and significant dates to barns, houses, furniture, and pottery.

The Dutch in rural New York followed their traditions in the stone houses they built. In towns, Dutch houses were typically made of brick, tall and narrow, with the gable end facing the street. Dutch interiors were enlivened by colorful tiles, textiles, brass, copper, and other furnishings popular in the Netherlands. Dutch interiors were enlivened by colorful tiles, textiles, brass, copper, and other furnishings popular in the Netherlands.

The Quakers, who were generally well-to-do, showed a preference for fine materials—walnut furniture and silk clothing—and for fashionable forms, but chose to eliminate much extravagant embellishment for religious reasons. Simplicity of manner, appearance, speech, and home was important to the Society of Friends, as were pacifism, education, and the belief that men and women were relatively equal. Quaker craftsmen tended to be conservative, preferring to continue making items in older styles, rather than quickly adopting each new fashion.

It was the cultural diversity of the middle colonies, as well as their key location between the colonies of New England and the South, that proved of value as the colonial period came to an end. By the time of the Revolution, people in New York, Pennsylvania, Maryland, and the other middle colonies had already gained considerable experience in learning how to resolve their differences and live together peaceably. These people were the link and the bridge in the new nation.

preceding pages:

A center-chimney log house at the Pennsylvania Farm Museum in Lancaster, Pennsylvania, was reconstructed in recent years, based on surviving examples from mid-eighteenth-century Lancaster County. The house's plan differs somewhat from those of New England center-chimney houses. Here, the downstairs is divided into a kitchen on one side—like the New England hall—but instead of a parlor on the other side there are two small sleeping rooms. The loft was used for storage and additional sleeping quarters. Log construction, instead of the English post-and-beam tradition, was characteristic of colonial Pennsylvania houses built by settlers of German background.

A detail of the bake oven at the Pennsylvania Farm Museum shows the red clay roof tiles distinctive to this area and other places where Germans settled. Tile roofs are heavy, but had the advantage of being fireproof. This small building, a reconstruction, also serves as a smokehouse to preserve meats. Colonial German-Americans usually built their ovens outdoors, while New England colonists usually incorporated them into the kitchen.

148

The house that Peter Wentz, Jr., built in 1758 on his farm in Worcester, Pennsylvania, combined Georgian and Pennsylvania-German building traditions. The symmetrical façade and center hall plan are Georgian. The pent eaves between stories, the use of fieldstone on the back and sides (with dressed stone on the front), and the paint-decorated shutters have German roots. The shutters were repainted white with black outlines highlighting the panels to match the original color scheme.

The summer kitchen in the ell off the back of the Peter Wentz House is separated from the main house by a breezeway with an arched opening. The location of the pump is probably original; it would have been handy to the kitchen. The hollowed sandstone trough is early; the pump itself is a replacement.

Wright's Ferry Mansion was built in 1738 in Columbia, Pennsylvania, ten miles from Lancaster. The house belonged to Susanna Wright, an English Quaker who came to Pennsylvania in 1714 with her family. A woman of intellect and independent spirit, she believed that men and women were equals.

Typical of the Georgian style as interpreted by the English Quakers in Pennsylvania are the pent eaves between the first and second stories, the placement of the windows, and the cove cornice. The house's proportions—long and narrow—are also common in early houses in the Philadelphia area.

Philipsburg Manor in North Tarrytown, New York, was
important in the late seventeenth and early eighteenth
centuries as a trading and milling center. The buildings
here are called the Upper Mills. The gambrel roof and
basic boxlike shape characterize Dutch-American
buildings of this type in the colonies.

The kitchen mantel at Wright's Ferry Mansion, simply constructed of a board and small brackets, was intended for use, not for style. It serves here as a storage place for pewter dishes and other small household objects, including an hourglass to time cooking and a bell.

On the tabletop are a large bowl and covered pot made of earthenware and decorated with lines and dots of "slip," or clay in liquid form. The tall brass pot with the handle jutting out from the side is a chocolate pot or coffeepot.

154

A staircase in the kitchen of Susanna Wright's mansion
leads up to quarters for the servants. It is much plainer
than the stylish staircase in the entry hall with its
boldly turned balusters. A well-placed window brings
light to the stairs.

The Peter Wentz House in Worcester, Pennsylvania, has two kitchens: this, the winter kitchen, and the summer kitchen in an ell on the back of the house.

The painted spots on the plaster wall are the most eye-catching feature of the winter kitchen. Most of the rest of the house is also gaily painted on the dadoes below the chair rail. The painted decoration was discovered and reapplied during the house's restoration.

preceding pages:

The dining room chamber, or the room above the dining room, in the Peter Wentz House features a bright blue paneled fireplace wall with salmon paint on the inside. These colors reproduce the originals, based on paint analysis. According to local tradition, the owners added only one coat of paint to this room since 1777, the year George Washington used it as a temporary headquarters.

The decorative paint on the dadoes beneath the chair rail has also been reapplied; a section of the original wall appears on the right. The wall features built-in cupboards and drawers, unusual amenities in the colonial period. This fireplace is a nineteenth-century replacement; the rest of the wall, including all the paneling, is original. On the hearth are a tin carrier for coal and a copper teakettle made by John Getz, a Pennsylvania coppersmith.

The Dutch tradition of making large molded cookies of Saint Nicholas at Christmastime is preserved at Philipsburg Manor in North Tarrytown, New York. The dough is pressed into a carved wooden mold made in Holland sometime between 1700 and 1750, then baked, and finally decorated with colors and gilding. The oak table is also Dutch.

The fireplace wall in the main bedchamber at Wright's Ferry Mansion in Pennsylvania is unpainted poplar. It, too, houses closets. The slat-back armchair is a commode, or potty-chair; the scalloped apron conceals the pewter chamber pot inside. It dates from about 1750, and its sharply graduated slats are particularly pleasing. The wrought-iron candlestand is especially nicely designed; it was made in Pennsylvania, probably in or around Philadelphia, and dates from the first half of the eighteenth century. The andirons are the room's earliest feature; they were made about 1690 and are fine examples of the William and Mary style in iron and brass work.

165

An unknown builder constructed this house on a lot in Annapolis, Maryland, that William Paca purchased immediately after his wedding to Ann Mary Chew in 1763. An attorney, Paca was later one of the signers of the Declaration of Independence and was elected governor of Maryland in 1782. The Pacas were Quakers, and so chose to build and furnish with relative simplicity for people of their station.

As in most buildings in the southern colonies, the main floor is raised above ground level. The façade also shows the symmetry that marked American houses in the Georgian-Palladian style. The stairs to the main entrance with the simple point finials on the posts have been reconstructed, based on archaeological evidence and some comparable examples in Annapolis.

A side view of the stairs on the façade of the Paca House shows the stone foundation and the louvered windows of the cellar level, which is accessible by stairs descending under the entry porch.

The fancifully named Bachelor's Hope was built sometime between 1753 and 1790, probably by William Hammersley, in Chaptico, Maryland. It is a most unusual example of Maryland architecture of this period. Its most distinctive features include the front portico, the hipped gable roof, and the angled roof lines of the wings, which extend up to meet the center section.

The central part of the house has one large ground-floor room. The brick wings on either side each have two rooms in a single story.

A closer view of the portico at Bachelor's Hope shows the ornamental cornice above the columns and the enclosed stairs that lead up to the main floor.

The gable end and chimney of Ocean Hall, built in the very early eighteenth century in Bushwood, Maryland, show one way of using brick in the colonies. The peaked outline of the roof of a former addition remains visible in the brickwork where it was later infilled. Although the house was built in the late seventeenth century, it was altered in the early eighteenth century when the interior was completely redesigned.

The house's most distinctive feature is a rare example of the upper-cruck roof in this country, that is, pairs of curved roof timbers supporting the framing. The cruck technique is ancient and was also used in the New World at Plimoth Plantation in the hovel (see page 24) built some fifty years earlier than this.

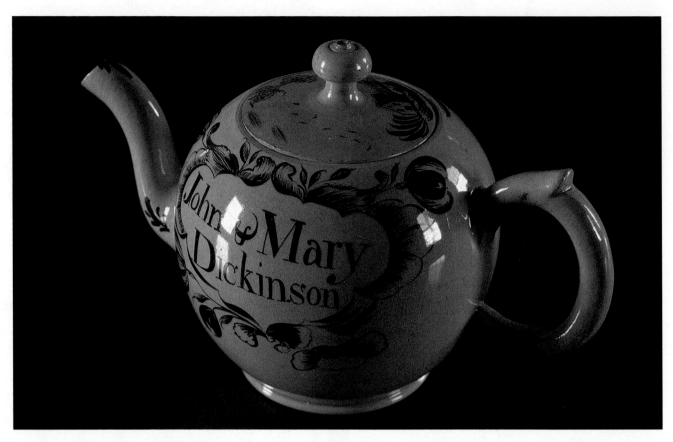

A small, white creamware teapot made in England was decorated to order especially for John Dickinson and Mary Norris, who married in 1770. The compact, round shape of the teapot is typical of the period. Today it remains in Poplar Hall, Kent County, Delaware.

This handsomely made mahogany "six-pack" carrier saved steps for a servant bringing bottles of ale or wine from the cellar. Dating from the late eighteenth century and probably made in America, it is similar in form to commonly used knife carriers and desk trays for paper, pens, and ink. The carrier is at the Hammond-Harwood House in Annapolis, Maryland.

Windsor chairs were one of the most popular forms of seating in eighteenth-century America. They were used by people in all walks of life. Windsor chairs are characterized by solid plank seats into which legs are inserted, and by spindles that form the back. This particular chair, at the Hammond-Harwood House in Annapolis, Maryland, follows a sack-back style: the crest rail is steamed and bent into a bow shape. Above the crest rail is a comb extension. This form is very rare.

The main stairs of the Paca House also show the Chinese influence in the trellis-pattern balustrade that leads from the second floor to the attic. As a young attorney, William Paca spent time in London, where he would have seen the stylish Chinese taste as interpreted by English designers.

The house at Sotterley Plantation in St. Mary's County, Maryland, evolved during the first quarter of the eighteenth century into an elongated one-and-a-half-story frame house. One of its grandest features is the Chinese Chippendale stair rail in the main hall. The squared trellises are based on examples of Chinese architecture, as interpreted in England before reaching the colonies. This and other interior woodwork has been attributed to Richard Boulton.

178

Few American colonial toys are as well documented as
this large wooden doll, now at the Hammond-Harwood
House in Annapolis. She belonged to Ann Proctor of
Baltimore, and had the distinction of having her
portrait painted along with Ann's by Charles Willson
Peale in 1789. The portrait is also at the Hammond-
Harwood House. Her arms have been replaced, but she
has her original wooden torso, stuffed kid legs and hair.
Her cap is a replica of the one in the painting, and she
sits in a chair that is nearly identical to the one in
which her young owner posed.

A tobacco barn near Tracey's Landing in Maryland dates from sometime around 1750. Its distinctive shape, with a shed on each side, is characteristic of barns in this area at the time.

The primitive interior of a slave cabin at Sotterley, a plantation in St. Mary's County, Maryland, forms a stark contrast with the fine homes in the colonies.

Here, the single downstairs room is furnished with a crudely made bed and benches. The stairs lead to a loft and additional sleeping space. There was probably little need for storage space; the people who lived here did not have many possessions. For privacy, separate sleeping areas could be made downstairs by hanging blankets from the ceiling.

186

A tall-case clock in the Paca House in Annapolis is crowned by an exuberant assemblage of carved details, including a molded broken-scroll pediment with carved rosettes, a pair of flame finials, and a Rococo cartouche in the center. The clock was made circa 1765–75 in Philadelphia; Edward Duffield made the works, and it is likely that the case also was made in his shop. The clock's silvered brass face shows the changing phases of the moon.

188

THE SOUTH

THE southern colonies included both the earliest and the latest settlements of the colonial period. The earliest included Sir Walter Raleigh's "Lost Colony," on Roanoke Island off the North Carolina coast, where 150 colonists disappeared without a trace, leaving nothing but the word *Croatan* (the name of a local Indian tribe) carved on a tree for a landing party to discover in 1589. Several other attempts at colonization were made, but none was successful until 1607, when Jamestown was established in Virginia. The last American colony to be established was Georgia, which was conceived in 1732 by James Oglethorpe in part as a place where people in debtors' prison in England could start a new life. Southern colonial settlements ranged from coastal and tidewater ports to backwoods, or piedmont, frontier farms from Virginia to southern Georgia. Southern colonists ranged from wealthy planters to indentured servants, slaves, and buccaneers.

The history of colonial Virginia, named for Elizabeth I, the "Virgin Queen," began when 105 men on three ships sailed up the James River and landed at a place they called Jamestown. They were sent by the Virginia Company in London under the leadership of Capt. John Smith, a soldier of fortune. The men had signed up for seven years' service to pay for their passage, and were sent to find gold and a water route to China. They had no idea how vast an unexplored continent lay to the west. The coast itself was hardly known. Capt. Smith complained, "I have had six or seven different maps of those Northern parts, so unlike each to other, and most so differing from any proportion of resemblance of the Country, they did me no more good than so much waste paper, though they cost me more."

The colony foundered, despite the arrival of additional men. Disease, starvation, and Indian attack decimated the early settlers: of the first seven hundred or eight hundred settlers, only sixty lived through the first three years.

King James I revoked the company's charter and claimed Virginia as a royal colony only a few years after it was established. With the passage of time, more colonists came, making their way up the James River and into the country around Albemarle Sound. Settlement was slow. Ninety years after the landing at Jamestown, a commentator said that Virginia "looks all like a wild desart; the high-lands overgrown with trees, and the low-lands sunk with water, marsh, and swamp . . . perhaps not the hundredth part of the country is yet clear'd from the woods, and not one foot of the marsh and swamp drained." Some very large plantations were established, which grew "sotweed," or tobacco, as a valuable cash crop, but for every large plantation, there were scores of small, isolated subsistence-level farms, worked by men and women who wore homespun and buckskin. Church and state in Virginia were one. The rites, services, and charitable works of the Anglican church were central to society. Towns, as they existed in New England and the middle colonies, were rare. Williamsburg was designated the capital in 1699. It grew into an elegant town, replacing Jamestown as the center of political, religious, social, and commercial life. George Washington, Thomas Jefferson, and Patrick Henry were among those who walked along its streets.

There were two centers of British settlement south of Virginia, both in Carolina, the colony named for King Charles II, who gave all the land between Virginia and the Spanish settlements in Florida to eight friends. Settlement of the northern region began in the 1650s, when farmers, trappers, merchants, and Indian traders moved in from Virginia and neighboring colonies. By 1700, a cluster of settlements had formed around Albemarle Sound. New groups came: Huguenots, Swiss, Germans, and others, many of them religious dissidents seeking refuge in the new colony, where they grew tobacco and raised cattle and other livestock. As in Virginia, there were few towns of any size. Some other colonists looked down at these backwoods settlers. William Byrd of Virginia related that the women "spin, weave and knit, all with their own hands, while their husbands, depending on the bounty of the climate, are slothful in everything but getting of children, and in only that instance make themselves useful members of an infant colony."

Life was different in the southern region of Carolina. Here, in 1670, Charles Town (later Charleston) was established at the juncture of the Ashley and Cooper rivers. It was at first a small but very prosperous community. Most colonists were wealthy Englishmen, some of whom had tried colonial life first in the West Indies. In 1679, Charleston became the capital. Its broad streets were laid out in an orderly pattern; planters received lots in town in proportion to the size of their plantations. Soon, Huguenots and Scots added to the population. By 1703, Charleston was the southernmost British settlement in North America, with slightly over 7,000 residents. Half of these were black slaves, Indians, or white indentured servants.

By the 1690s, it was clear that the southern and northern regions of Carolina were really separate entities. The separation was formalized in 1729.

Georgia was the last of the original thirteen colonies to be established. It was the only one that was not begun in the seventeenth century. It was the enterprise of James Oglethorpe, a member of Parliament, who won the support of King George II for his proposal that debtors be allowed to settle the land between South Carolina and the Spanish holdings in Florida. Oglethorpe had high hopes for his colony, where no settler was to own more than five hundred acres, and where slavery and liquor were banned.

In 1733, 114 settlers arrived at the mouth of the Savannah River after a brief stop in Charleston. Oglethorpe and a scouting party searched for a defensible location for a settlement, choosing a hill on the Savannah River about twenty miles inland. The settlers went to work building a town named for the river. Like Charleston, Savannah was laid out in an orderly plan. Settlers had a home plot, a garden plot at the edge of town, and farmland beyond the town limits. Their plans were to raise silkworms and grapes, but they found that tobacco was a more successful enterprise. Other settlements were to be modeled on Savannah as more colonists arrived.

The early dwellings of the southern colonies varied widely from elegant plantation mansions to one-room houses. The typical house of the dirt farmer was dark and drafty and had a dirt floor. It was commonly not maintained, because it was a temporary shelter, to be abandoned when tobacco exhausted the soil. Scattered throughout the region were large plantation houses, modeled on the vast country houses on estates in England. One observer commented, "They always contrive to have large rooms, that they may be cool in Summer. . . . All their Drudgeries of Cookery, Washing, Daries, &c. are perform'd in Offices detacht from the Dwelling-House, which by this means are kept more cool and Sweet."

Charleston, the only metropolis south of Philadelphia, glittered as the social and commercial center of the southern colonies. Planters from the outlying estates moved for the summer to their elegant town houses with lacy iron gates and balconies, where they could enjoy cool sea breezes. In 1773, the city impressed Josiah Quincy, a Boston Yankee, who described a room in one of these residences as the "grandest hall I ever beheld, azure blue satin window curtains, rich blue paper with gilt, mashee borders, most elegant pictures."

In the Moravian settlement in North Carolina, devout colonists perpetuated German traditions in building, dressing, and daily life. They lined the streets of Salem with neat, well-built half-timbered shops and dwellings. The town was begun in 1766 after a decade of developing farmland in the area. It was the center of a thriving commercial life, with large numbers of highly skilled craftsmen and merchants. Elsewhere in North Carolina, there were few plantations and no large urban centers. Royal Governor William Tryon's "palace" in New Bern formed an astonishing contrast with the scattered settlement farmhouses.

Wealthy southern colonists looked to England for models of what was fashionable. London, not Philadelphia, New York, or

Boston, was the style center. Wealthy southern colonists imported vast quantities of fine furniture from London. Local cabinetmakers used these as models to produce very similar works in local woods, especially walnut, some fruitwoods, and yellow pine, used as a secondary wood. Charleston and Williamsburg cabinetmakers used imported mahogany for more costly pieces. The best-known cabinetmaker in early Charleston, Thomas Elfe, was English by birth and training. Charleston was the chief cabinetmaking center in the South. Well-to-do colonists also ordered furniture from stylish workshops in Boston and other New England centers. Shiploads of furniture traveled to southern ports.

As in New England and the middle colonies, life in the southern colonies was marked by contrast, as civilization mingled with the frontier. While Charleston and Savannah grew into sophisticated ports, and plantations developed along the rivers, backwoods people eked out a simple living. In spite of the contrasts, southern colonists formed a strong core of patriots and leaders. When the Revolution came, poor farmers and wealthy plantation owners joined forces to establish a common front against the power of the Crown.

196

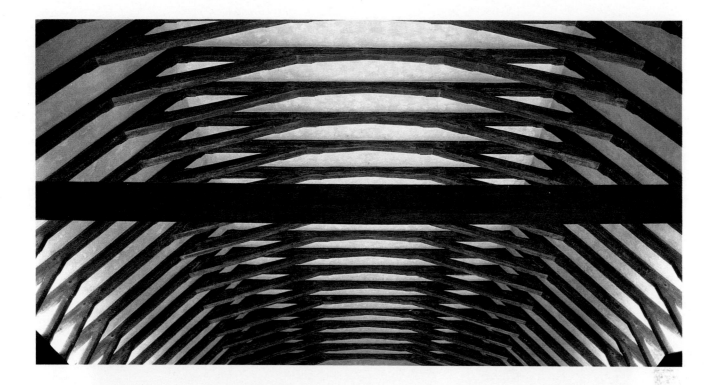

St. Luke's Church, near Smithfield, Virginia, is the
nation's only original Gothic church. It was begun in
1632. The interior may have been completed as long as
twenty-five years later. The roof was designed so that
the church's interior would be uninterrupted by pillars.
This is a view of the Gothic tie-beam timber roof. The
timbers are chamfered and decorated with lamb's-
tongue moldings. The church was extensively restored
in the 1950s. This is an exact replica of the original roof.
By good luck, workers found the lines of the original
timbers traced against the west wall of the nave when
they removed later plaster.

The baptismal font in St. Luke's Church was hewn
from a section of a large tree trunk. It holds a silver
baptismal basin attributed to Jacob Boelen, a silversmith in the colonies.

198

Bacon's Castle was built in Surrey County, Virginia, circa 1655. It is a rare surviving example of the English Jacobean style in the colonies. Typical of this style are the clustered chimneys and the Baroque gabled end. Each flue in the chimney group is from a different fireplace opening.

The house at Shirley Plantation near Charles City, Virginia, was probably built by John Carter shortly after his wedding in 1723. Carter was a merchant and planter, as well as a government official. Tobacco was his primary crop. Fine interior details indicate the wealth and refinement of the family.

This broken-arch pediment is over the doorway of the parlor, which Charles Carter, John's son, used as a dining room for his large family. The pineapple echoes the large decorative pineapple at the peak of the roof. This pediment was probably added by the younger Carter after he moved to Shirley in 1771. It has been a source of inspiration to restoration architects, including those at Colonial Williamsburg.

The concept of home in the colonial period included outbuildings as well as the main dwelling house. Such buildings might include kitchens, dairies, corncribs, and stables.

Here are some of the outbuildings reconstructed at the George Wythe House in Williamsburg, including a kitchen, laundry, and lumber or storage house. The outbuildings range along the property line paralleling Prince George Street, a side street in town, and define one side of a domestic yard to the rear of the house.

Some shutters in Williamsburg are painted chocolate, or dark brown. These are made of two boards joined with three horizontal battens and wrought nails. They are hung on pintels and held open by "iron dogs" made of wrought iron.

A Williamsburg craftsman fits together the rough-sawn pieces of a Chippendale style chair: two posts, the crest rail at the top of the back, and the splat in the center of the back. These pieces will then be disassembled, carved to finished shape, and reassembled.

A craftsman at Williamsburg shapes a furniture leg, working it after the piece has been turned on the lathe. The bottom of the leg has a pad foot.

The cabinetmaker shapes the crest rail of a chair in the Chippendale style with a tool called a spokeshave, chamfering it to give it a rounded edge.

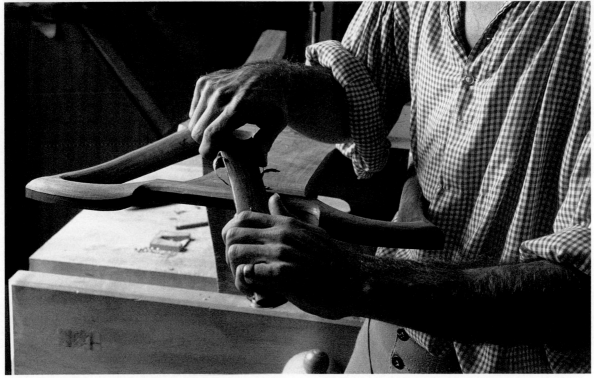

The cabriole leg, characterized by its S shape, was popular on furniture made in the eighteenth century. The basic shape is sawn, then rounded with a spokeshave or drawknife. The claw-and-ball foot was carved. These popular feet were simply called claw feet in the eighteenth century. The shell carving on the knee requires the maker to leave enough extra wood when doing the first rough cutting to allow for carving in relief. The work here was done in Williamsburg's cabinetmaking shop.

Another kind of cabriole leg terminates in a pad foot,
a style that was simpler and required less time and
expertise.

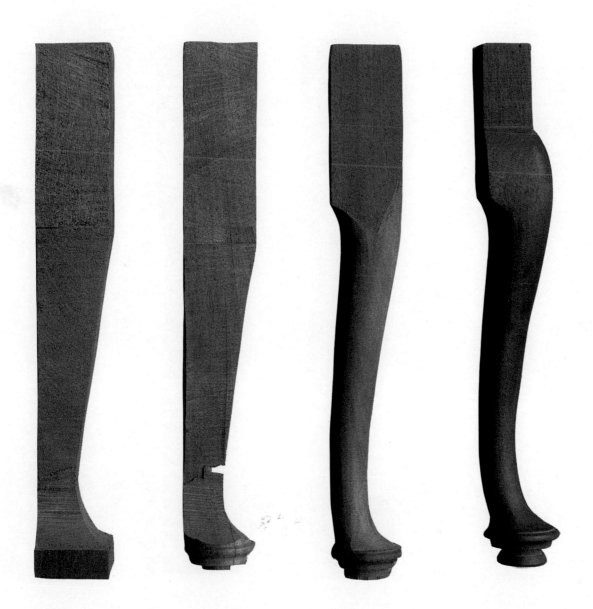

Another view of the Anthony Hay cabinetmaking shop
shows several workbenches: one very handsomely
made, with drawers and cupboards, and two that are
far more crude. Near the workbenches is a selection of
chisels for carving, cutting, and shaping wood on the
lathe.

In production are the base for a stand with claw-and-
ball feet, a chair in the Chippendale style, and the crest
for a high chest. On the middle workbench are leg
patterns. The simply made work stools contrast vividly
with the elegant and elaborately decorative chair being
made.

The carved pediment of a desk and bookcase has been
reproduced by one of Williamsburg's skilled craftsmen.
It is copied from a desk and bookcase made circa
1765–70 by a worker in Anthony Hay's cabinetmaking
shop in Williamsburg. The pediment reflects the
appreciation of Classical structures as understood in the
colonies by way of England.

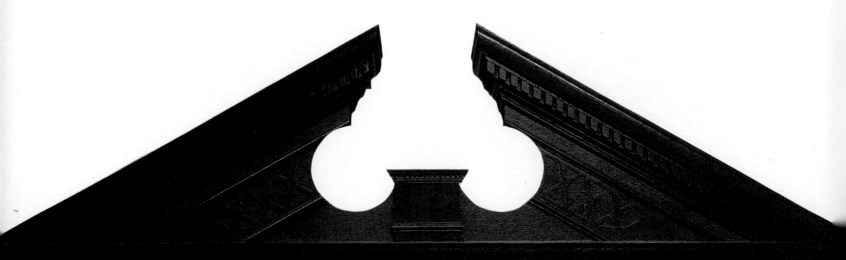

Williamsburg had a number of cabinetmaking shops in the colonial period. About a dozen cabinetmakers have been documented as having lived in the town in the eighteenth century. The two major shops belonged to Anthony Hay and Peter Scott.

Today, highly skilled craftsmen reproduce furniture in a reconstruction of Hay's shop. Here, a cabinetmaker works on carving a finial for the central plinth of the pediment for the desk and bookcase.

This corner cupboard from Accomack County, Virginia, has many associations with the architecture on the Eastern Shore of Virginia in the eighteenth century. The moldings on the doors, applied pilasters, and complex paneling on the piece are familiar architectural elements in houses in the area. The practice of highlighting moldings and other elements with a contrasting paint color is common in Eastern Shore furniture. The tricolor cornice is especially pleasing.

Court cupboards are among the most imposing pieces of seventeenth-century furniture. This form, which was used in the royal courts of the Old World, combines a cabinet with drawers and an open shelf for display of important and valuable possessions. This example features an open shelf at the top, in contrast to New England examples, in which it is usually located at the bottom. The bosses, or oval medallions, split spindles, and turned baluster supports are of walnut, painted black to simulate ebony, a costlier wood. This cupboard descended from Thomas Vines of York County, Virginia, and was probably made circa 1640. It is now in the Museum of Early Southern Decorative Arts in Winston-Salem, North Carolina.

When the Moravian Single Brothers' Workshop was
built in 1771, Salem was an important commercial and
trading center. The building housed workshops for
important industries, and included a bakery, weaving
room, hatter's shop and joinery. A single master
directed activity in each of the workshops, assisted by
journeymen and apprentices. The building was constructed from logs, with a half-timbered section
in the middle.

The original structure was torn down in 1921. This
building is a reconstruction on the original site.

234

233

preceding pages:

Each evening the Single Brothers gathered in the hall or saal for vespers at the end of the workday and again to sing for an hour before going to bed. Like all Moravian worship halls of this period, it is simply furnished. At the left is the table from which the speaker read from the Bible. The table is surrounded by a plain green skirt; the top is covered with leather. The Brothers sat on the plainest of benches. The room's simplicity sets off the two pieces that combine utility with a degree of magnificence: the organ with tracker action to the left, built in 1797–98 by David Tannenberg, from Lititz, Pennsylvania, another Moravian community, and the large glazed earthenware tile stove to the right. The stove is a reproduction made using old molds.

Behind the table is a painting by John Ballentine Haidt, circa 1760, that depicts Mary, Jesus, and John the Baptist. It is largely from Haidt's portraits that we know about the clothing worn by eighteenth-century Moravians.

In the tavern built in 1784 in Old Salem, a piece of meat suspended by a string cooks over an earthenware pan to catch the drips. This method of preparing meat was not uncommon. In *American Cookery*, written in 1796, Amelia Simmons tells readers "to hang down rather than to spit" in her directions for roasting beef.

238

This downstairs dining room in the Salem Tavern was reserved for the use of gentlemen who lodged in the rooms above. Across the hall was the public room, right, for less distinguished guests. There, a standard meal was served for a fixed price at the same time daily. In the gentlemen's dining room, visitors could dine at a time of their choosing.

241

For the Moravians, work was a form of worship, a way of serving God. The congregation owned and operated five major businesses: a tannery, pottery, general store, mill, and tavern. Other craftsmen followed other trades, more or less on their own, although under the supervision of the church.

Each business was managed by a single master, assisted by journeymen and apprentices. This system eliminated competition between major trade groups.

Here, coopers' compasses hang on the wall. Coopers, who produced barrels, pails, tubs, and other items made by joining wooden staves with iron or wooden hoops, used the compasses to make circles for barrel and pail bottoms and lids.

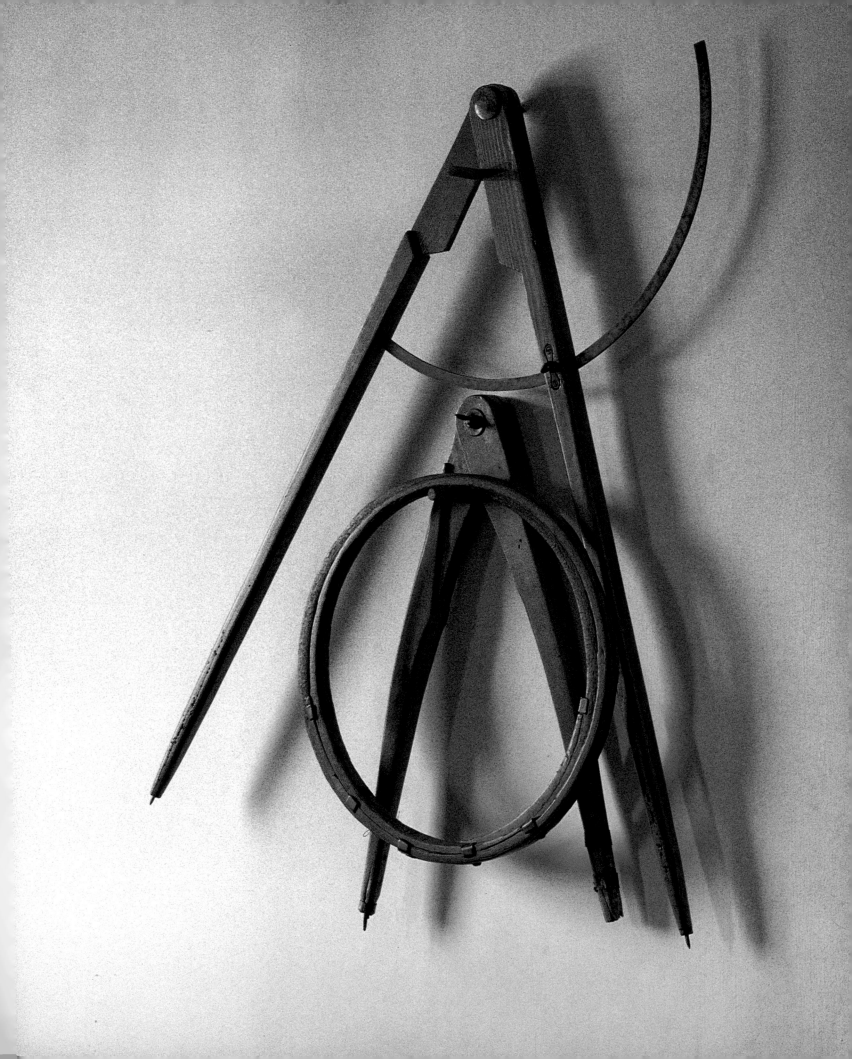

Colonial American women with sufficient time and
energy made decorative needlework to brighten their
clothing and homes. Crewel work was used for
bedhangings, petticoat borders, and detachable pockets
that tied around the waist. This is a typical floral
design stitched with woolen thread on linen.

Moravian clothing was typical of what was worn by other colonists, but plainer. Shiny buttons and shoe buckles were frowned on. A haube, or cap, distinguished Moravian women from nonbelievers.

In the eighteenth century, Moravians made most of their own clothing. Here, in a tailor's shop, shirt and trousers are being made. A paper pattern lies under the shears on the worktable in the foreground.

246

247

Two graceful wrought-iron rat-tail hinges affix the door to this walnut map cupboard, now in the Old Salem collections. The rat-tail hinge enables the door to be easily removed when one is moving the piece, and thus has a functional purpose in addition to being a pleasing form.

The rat-tail hinge has its roots in European furniture, and is fairly common on Moravian furniture made in the eighteenth century.

Bargello or flamestitch, often in bold color combinations, was a form of needlepoint used on upholstered easy chairs, gentlemen's pocketbooks, and small ornamental sewing accessories such as pincushions.

preceding pages:

Gate-leg tables with turned supports and drop leaves were made in many sizes during the colonial period. The size of the leaves determined the number of gates needed for support. This table, made of walnut in Charleston, South Carolina, circa 1710, has an extra leg under the gates, a feature frequently found on northern gate legs, but extremely unusual on southern examples. Perhaps the unidentified maker had lived or traveled in the northern colonies. The table is now in the Museum of Early Southern Decorative Arts in Winston-Salem, North Carolina.

The doorway woodwork on the north wall of the dining room in Tryon Palace in New Bern, North Carolina, is from Weald Hall, Brentwood, in Essex, England. It faces an exterior door, not visible here, which leads to the Trent River. Centered on the dining room table is a silver epergne, made by the London silversmith William Cripps sometime between 1751 and 1775, surrounded by four Irish silver candlesticks made by William Ward of Dublin between 1770 and 1780.

In the mid-eighteenth century, Charleston was the largest urban center south of Philadelphia, and home to some of the finest cabinetmakers in America. This library bookcase, made in Charleston circa 1770 and attributed to the workshop of Thomas Elfe, is an adaptation of a design from Thomas Chippendale's *The Gentleman and Cabinet-Maker's Director*. This book, published in 1755, combined classical, Chinese, French Rococo, and other motifs to create the Chippendale style. The maker copied Chippendale's design almost exactly but raised the base higher and turned the four inlaid ovals across the front up on edge. The bookcase is now in the Museum of Early Southern Decorative Arts.

Drayton Hall, near Charleston, was built by
John Drayton, whose father, Thomas, was the first
of his family to settle in America. He arrived in 1679,
after a period in Barbados.

In 1738, John Drayton bought land adjoining his
father's estate and began to build Drayton Hall, which
was completed in 1742. He was vastly wealthy; Drayton
Hall was only one of more than thirty properties that he
owned during his lifetime. The plantation around
Drayton Hall had more than 700 acres. The family
originally lived here except for the winter social season,
which they spent in Charleston. By the time of the
Revolution, the Draytons, like other families of means,
spent the hot weather in the mountains or along the
coast, using the hall only in spring and summer.

In all, seven generations of Draytons used this hall. It
remains in a remarkably original state. Because the
family used the hall so little in the late nineteenth and
twentieth centuries, they preferred to preserve it much
as it was when built and occupied regularly. The family
never added running water, electric lighting, or central
heating. Parts of the house retain their first coat of
eighteenth-century paint.

263

The great hall on the second floor of Drayton Hall, also
called the ballroom, has a ceiling that is fourteen feet
high. The coat of arms in the overmantel was painted
by a member of the Drayton family in the 1930s. The
Latin motto, *Hac Iter Ad Astra*, means "This road (or
way) to the stars." (*Hac* is a variant spelling of the more
usual *Haec*.) This view looks out to the landward
portico.

The double stairs in Drayton Hall were made from
mahogany imported from the West Indies. The stair
hall rises a magnificent twenty-seven feet.

264

A window seat in the northeast bedchamber of Drayton
Hall includes a most unusual feature: the seat lifts like a
lid to reveal a ledge underneath. This may have served
as a convenient place for a chamber pot, especially
since the small passageway can be made private by
closing the doors on both sides. Chamber pots were
usually kept under the bed. For primary use, there was
a seven-seat privy with paneled seats; one seat at each
end was short, for children, and the two seats in the
center were fitted with armrests. That structure is one
of the few surviving outbuildings on the plantation.

The service staircase at Drayton Hall goes directly from the basement to the attic. It is the only access to the attic. It provided the route for some household chores. The small stairs are very different from the grand stairs that members of the household and visitors used.

Here, the square hole cut for the household cat remains in the door to the attic, allowing it free access to the mice there.

In 1751, Ebenezer Wells added a grand new front to the old house behind, which he had built in 1717 in Deerfield, Massachusetts. The old house typifies seventeenth-century dwellings, with its random placement of door and windows, unpainted sheathing, small casement windows, and stone foundation. Its squat proportions convey a stoutness of construction that meant safety and comfort to its inhabitants.

In contrast, the new house rises balanced and stately from its brick foundation. Its façade is a model of symmetry, its clapboards are painted sky blue, and its sash windows bring much more light into the rooms.

The Wells-Thorn House dramatizes the changes that took place in a century and a half of colonial life. As people like Ebenezer Wells went about their day-to-day business, America changed from "a plain wilderness as God first made it" into a vigorous young nation, confident, competent, and ready to assert its independence.

Photo Credits

Paul Rocheleau:

15, 40, 58–59, 136, 137, 146–147, 149, 150, 151, 152, 153, 155, 156, 157, 158–159, 161, 163, 164–165, 167, 168, 169, 171, 172, 173, 175, 176 (both), 177, 179, 181, 182, 183, 184, 185, 186, 187, 188, 214, 215, 232–233, 234, 235, 236–237, 239, 240, 241, 243, 245, 246, 247, 248, 249, 250, 252–253, 254–255, 257, 259, 260, 261, 263, 264, 265, 266, 267

Michael Freeman:

4–5, 6–7, 21, 22–23, 24–25, 26–27, 28–29, 30, 31, 32, 33, 34, 35, 37, 38–39, 40–41, 43, 44–45, 46, 48–49 (both), 50–51, 52–53, 54–55, 56, 56–57, 61, 62, 63, 64, 65, 66, 67, 68–69, 70–71, 72, 73, 74, 75, 77, 78–79, 80, 81, 82–83, 85, 86–87, 89, 91, 92–93, 95, 97, 99, 100, 101, 102–103, 104–105, 106, 107, 109, 110–111, 113, 114–115, 117, 119, 121, 123, 124, 125, 126, 127, 128, 129, 130–131, 133, 134, 135, 189, 196, 197, 198, 199, 200, 201, 202, 203, 204–205, 206, 207 (both), 208, 209, 210–211, 212, 213, 216, 216–217, 218, 219, 221, 223, 224, 225, 226–227, 229, 268–269

David Larkin:

47, 230, 231, 268

Colonial Williamsburg Foundation:

244, 251

Connecticut Historical Society:

112

Acknowledgments

For their gracious and generous guidance, insights, and time, we are deeply grateful to Abbott Lowell Cummings, Cary Carson, Alice Winchester, Phil Zea, and Sumpter T. Priddy III. They have richly contributed to this book.

We are also grateful to those who assisted in many ways:

Barbara Allston-Brand	Susan Lisk
Jeremy Bangs	Paula Locklair
Sally Bromage	Joanna McBrien
Joseph Butler	Elizabeth McLoughlin
Curtis Campbell	Audrey Michie
Ed Chase	Mrs. James Newton
George Clark	Richard Nylander
Nancy Curtis	Karin Peterson
Mrs. Henry Edmonds	Wally Prisby
Mark Edwards	Orlando Ridout V
Letitia Galbraith	Meg Schaefer
Elizabeth Gamon and the late Albert Gamon	David Shields
Suzanne Goucher	Robert Sieber
Bernard Herman	Pringle Simmons
Frank Horton	June Tilton
David Kayser	Richard Trask
Doug Kendall	Connie Wyrick
Elizabeth Kirschner	

The writers warmly thank Harold and Florie Corbin, who looked at hundreds of slides at the beginning; and also Jim and Bitsy Harley, who gave us hospitality and a comfortable corner to write when we needed it most, at the end.

Finally, we are grateful to Leslie Stoker, our editor, for her grace, good sense, and patience; and to Andy Stewart for suggesting that the book be done.

270

Index

Pages in *italic* contain illustrations